Are you ever confused about what your child is learning at school? Do you sometimes wonder if they're doing as well as they should be? Does helping with their homework worry you?

If the answer to any of these questions is yes, then this guide is for you.

Gathered together in one handy book for the very first time, here is all the information you need to help your child get the best out of their first few years in play school, nursery and primary.

It explains exactly what schools teach and why, clears up the answers to some of the most common questions parents ask, and is packed full of useful tips to make learning fun in the car, at the park, on the bus and in the supermarket.

This little book can't answer all your questions about your child's education – some of them will need answering at their school, which will provide its own information about everything from uniforms to school lunches.

But it will equip you with all the information you need to help your child get the best start in learning.

You don't have to read it all at once: it's designed to be dipped into as and when. Care has been taken to include information that won't go out of date.

Using this guide

This guide is for reference, so there's no need to sit and read it all through at once. It's designed to be dipped into as your child grows from 3 to 7. It will come in useful, so keep it handy.

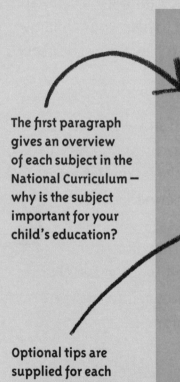

The first paragraph gives an overview of each subject in the National Curriculum — why is the subject important for your child's education?

Optional tips are supplied for each subject. These are fun activities that you might do with your child to support their learning. (You don't have to do the tips! See page 75 for more information.)

Music

Why do schools teach music?
We've all got our 'desert island discs', songs that remind us of places we've visited, or tunes that always cheer us up when we're feeling down. Making music together helps children to explore and express their thoughts and feelings. Learning songs from times gone by or from different parts of the world helps children learn about other times and other cultures. And getting to grips with listening carefully is going to help them in all sorts of different lessons throughout their school career.

TIP
Sing it with me

Most children love singing at this age. Give them lots of encouragement – singing is not only fun, but will give your child a sense of melody that will help their school work.

Some songs can also be very helpful for other subjects such as English and mathematics. Remembering songs – like 'Now I know my ABC' or '1, 2, 3, 4, 5, once I caught a fish alive' – can be great for helping your child learn the letters of the alphabet, or to count out numbers.

56

'Teaching for every child' explains what schools have to teach. 'Targets for every child' explains the target children will be aiming for, around age 7. See page 74 for more information.

aching for every child

ldren are taught how to sing and play musical instruments. They explore nds and create their own short compositions. They learn to listen carefully, ding out and describing how sounds can change: for example, getting her, lower, louder, quieter. They experience a wide range of music from erent times and cultures.

rgets for every child

und age 7, most children are able to:
sing songs from memory, knowing when the tune goes up and down
keep to a steady rhythm when singing and playing music
start making their own simple musical patterns, carefully choosing
different sounds
describe sounds using words such as 'high' and 'low', and by using
musical symbols
mprove their own work.

Music

Each subject in the guide has a colour-coded tab for easy reference, and begins on a new coloured page.

How the curriculum works

This section explains how the curriculum works. You will find it a helpful introduction to this book. At the end of the book (page 74) you will find answers to some other questions that parents often ask.

Schools keep in touch with parents regularly to explain important developments and will be able to answer any questions you have more fully. Your first contact for help is always your child's teacher.

What is the National Curriculum and why does it matter to parents?

The National Curriculum:

▷ sets out the most important knowledge and skills that every child has a right to learn

▷ is a framework given to teachers by government, so that all school children are taught in a way that is balanced and manageable, but hard enough to challenge them

▷ gives standards that measure how well children are doing in each subject – so teachers can plan to help them do better.

The National Curriculum isn't just for teachers and schools: it belongs to everyone. This book will help you understand it, so you can help your child as they begin their journey.

What is foundation stage, and why does it matter to parents?

The foundation stage happens before the National Curriculum: it is a framework for your child's learning in nursery or reception class. This book explains the areas of learning in the foundation stage on pages 12–17.

Stages, years, national tests and tasks

Age	Stage	Year	Tests
3–4	Foundation		
4–5		Reception	
5–6	Key stage 1	Year 1	
6–7		Year 2	National tests and tasks in English and maths
7–8	Key stage 2	Year 3	
8–9		Year 4	
9–10		Year 5	
10–11		Year 6	National tests in English, maths and science
11–12	Key stage 3	Year 7	
12–13		Year 8	
13–14		Year 9	National tests in English, maths and science
14–15	Key stage 4	Year 10	Some children take GCSEs
15–16		Year 11	Most children take GCSEs or other national qualifications

At the end of the National Curriculum key stages 1, 2 and 3 your child will sit national tests (popularly called 'SATs'). At the end of key stage 4 they will sit national examinations, often GCSEs.

I don't always follow talk about foundation stage, year 1, key stage, National Curriculum, tests and levels. How does it all work?

Find your child's age on the diagrams on pages 7 and 10, and you will be able to see what stage they are at in their learning — red highlights information covered in this book. At the end of this book you will find a 'teacher talk' section (pages 79–82) – this explains some key words in more detail.

The National Curriculum says when things must be taught by describing broad 'key stages'. Stages are blocks of years:

▷ foundation stage covers learning when your child is aged 3–5
▷ key stage 1 covers National Curriculum learning when your child is aged 5–7.

Key stage 1 lasts two years: schools are free to organise teaching within this time as they think best. They create their own plans, term by term and year by year.

What subjects are taught at key stage 1?

At key stage 1, all state schools have to teach all the National Curriculum subjects in this book:

▷ English
▷ mathematics
▷ science
▷ design and technology
▷ information and communication technology
▷ history
▷ geography
▷ art and design
▷ music
▷ physical education.

They also have to teach religious education.

This book also describes personal, social and health education and citizenship, which does not have to be taught – but many schools choose to teach it.

Not every subject will be taught in separate lessons. For more information, see page 76.

9

Key stages and National Curriculum levels

National Curriculum levels measure your child's progress in each subject. They are like the rungs of a ladder: children move up through the levels as they move up through the school.

	Key stage 1 (ages 5–7)	Key stage 2 (ages 7–11)	Key stage 3 (ages 11–14)
Level 8			
Level 7			
Level 6			
Level 5			
Level 4			
Level 3			
Level 2			
Level 1			

⊂══════⊃ During the key stage, most children will work within this range of levels.
━━━━━━━ By the end of the key stage, most children reach the target.

Notes
* *Not all children progress at the same rate. See page 74.*
* *The National Curriculum levels are not used for assessment at key stage 4.*

Other questions

There are lots of other questions parents ask about their child's learning. You may, for example, be worried about whether your child will reach the target for their age group, or about special educational needs.

There are answers to these questions at the end of this book, starting on page 74. But first, glance at the two main sections of this book, which describe what all children will be taught up to age 7. Both sections also offer some simple ideas about things you can do to support your child's learning when they are at home.

Learning for children aged 3–5

All 4 year olds and many 3 year olds are entitled to free part-time education. These early years, together with their time in reception class at primary school, make up the foundation stage.

It probably won't feel like learning – most children see it as just fun and play. But as they get to grips with speaking and listening, singing and dancing, stories and counting, they'll be gaining all the basic skills that will get them off to a flying start when they reach year 1.

What is the foundation stage?

It's for children aged 3–5, and covers the years they spend from the beginning of nursery or pre-school to the end of reception class in primary school. It's being introduced from September 2000 to cover these important years in your child's life.

Where will my child go for foundation stage?

The government is funding foundation stage places:

▷ in nursery and reception classes
▷ in playgroups
▷ in pre-schools
▷ in nurseries
▷ with accredited childminders in approved childminding networks.

To find out what's available in your area, call ChildcareLink on 08000 96 02 96, or look at their web site: http://www.childcarelink.gov.uk. ChildcareLink can give you the number of your local Children's Information Service, who will tell you what's available.

Wherever your child goes, staff who work with them will focus on the early learning goals.

What are the early learning goals?

They set out what most children are expected to achieve by the end of the foundation stage. They help people who work with children aged 3–5 to focus on what children need to learn. They are not a curriculum with lots of different subjects. They are six broad areas of learning.

▷ **Personal, social and emotional development**. Your child will learn to be self-confident, take an interest in things, know what their own needs are, tell the difference between right and wrong, and be able to dress and undress.

▷ **Communication, language and literacy**. Your child will learn to talk confidently and clearly, enjoying stories, songs and poems, hearing and saying sounds, and linking them to the alphabet. They will read and write some familiar words and learn to use a pencil.

▷ **Mathematical development**. Your child will develop an understanding of maths through stories, songs, games and imaginative play. They will become comfortable with numbers and with ideas such as 'heavier than' or 'bigger'. They will be aware of shapes and space.

▷ **Knowledge and understanding of the world**. Your child will explore and find out about the world around them, asking questions about it. They will build with different materials, know about everyday technology and learn what it is used for. They will find out about past events in their lives and their families' lives. They will find out about different cultures and beliefs.

▷ **Physical development**. Your child will learn to move confidently, controlling their body and handling equipment.

▷ **Creative development**. Your child will explore colours and shapes, trying out dance, making things, telling stories and making music.

Will the goals put pressure on my child?
No. Most of the time, children will feel they're just playing and having fun. Sometimes they'll choose what they want to do. Sometimes they'll take part in an activity that helps them learn how to concentrate or develop a particular skill, like using scissors or gluing card.

Will my child be tested at the end of the foundation stage?
No. And there's no cause for concern if your child moves forward faster in some areas than others.

What about when my child starts reception class?
When your child first starts reception class, their teacher carries out a baseline assessment, to find out about your child's learning needs. It's not a formal test. It's often done simply by doing some regular classroom activity with your child, such as looking at a book with them, so they won't even be aware they're being assessed. It's not something you or your child should worry about.

Can my child start earlier than four?
Quite possibly: the number of free part-time education places for 3 year olds is growing all the time. Contact the Children's Information Service (see page 13) to find out what's available.

What can I do to help my child?

You're probably doing it already! Finding out what they have done at nursery, discovering what they like and don't like, encouraging them to ask questions, listen to others and try out new skills all help support their learning process. Reading your child stories and helping them to learn nursery rhymes is particularly helpful.

Keep this book, ready for when your child starts at school in key stage 1, after the foundation stage. It is full of advice and tips about ways you can help your child, so you will want to look at them later. You don't have to do all (or any) of the tips, but any you can do will support your child's learning during key stage 1.

Teaching for children aged 5–7

These years of your child's time at school are called key stage 1.

At the end of each key stage, each National Curriculum subject has a target: your child should have reached a particular level of skills, knowledge and understanding.

Why have targets and tests?
▷ Children get a sense of achievement from reaching each milestone in their learning, and going beyond it.
▷ Schools use them to check on children's progress, so that they can match their teaching to each child's needs and abilities.
▷ The government uses them to see how many children are making the right kind of progress (especially in English and mathematics, where children take National Curriculum tests and tasks at age 7).

Of course, some children may not make as much progress as others and some have special educational needs. Please read the important information about this on page 74.

As a parent or carer, you have a very important role to play in helping your child learn. Some parents are afraid of doing the wrong thing. (If you are unsure about how to help, you can always ask your child's teacher.) The most important things you can do are:

▷ take an interest in what your child is learning at school, and encourage them to tell you about it
▷ praise them when they have done well.

There are other things you can do, too: this book also gives ideas and tips for each subject. Don't feel you have to do all of them, but any you can do will support your child's learning at school.

English

Why do schools teach English?

To get the most out of school, your child needs to get to grips with four basic skills – speaking, listening, reading and writing. This is what their English lessons are all about. These are where they learn how to express themselves clearly and creatively. They listen to and read stories and poems from all over the world, explore their imagination and read to find out facts.

TIP **Write it down!**

Writing useful messages and instructions is great practice for your child. Can they help you write your shopping list, or phone messages? How about writing instructions about how to look after the cat or dog? Cooking and writing down a recipe helps them to link words with flavours and smells (and to think about quantities, which strengthens their maths).

Children are taught:

▷ **speaking and listening**: they think about what they say, choose the right words, listen to others before they speak, talk with others and share ideas. They take different roles in drama, tell stories, read aloud, and describe events and experiences

▷ **reading**: they focus on words and sentences and how they fit into whole texts. Children work out the meaning of what they read and say why they like it or why they don't. They read stories, plays, poems, information texts in print and on computer screens, and use dictionaries and encyclopaedias

▷ **writing**: they compose stories, poems, notes, lists, captions, records, messages and instructions. They learn how to use punctuation to show the meaning of sentences, practise clear handwriting, and discover that thinking about patterns of letters and sounds helps them to spell words correctly.

The literacy hour
Nearly all schools use the *National Literacy Strategy: Framework for teaching*. This gives detailed aims for teaching reading and writing. These are taught during a daily literacy hour for all pupils.

Targets for every child

Around age 7, most children are able to:

Speaking and listening
▷ listen carefully
▷ show they have thought about listeners by including details to interest them
▷ speak clearly
▷ tell stories, and repeat rhymes and poems
▷ learn new words and use them in conversation
▷ change how they talk to different people, in a range of situations.

Reading
▷ give their views about events or ideas in what they read
▷ read aloud and understand stories and information books
▷ use more than one way to work out the meaning of unfamiliar words.

Writing
▷ write stories with a beginning, a middle and an end
▷ use writing for different purposes, such as lists or instructions
▷ use interesting vocabulary that suits the subject
▷ choose words and details to interest the reader
▷ write in sentences, using capital letters at the beginning and full stops at the end
▷ spell familiar words correctly
▷ use spelling patterns to write unfamiliar words
▷ shape letters correctly and write neatly and clearly.

TIP Listen!

Take a few moments to listen to different sounds with your child (perhaps the sound of rain, wind, sirens or aeroplanes).

Pick out one of the sounds – can your child describe it in words? Encourage them to describe it in different ways. At first they might say 'it was loud' or 'it was quiet', but the harder they listen, the more they might be able to add other descriptions: 'it was low and growly … it sounded slow'.

Switch on the radio: can they talk about the sound of voices in the same way?

TIP Hidden words

Put junk mail to good use. Pick out leaflets with large, bright lettering and get your child to find smaller words in bigger ones. For example, they can find the word 'live' in 'delivery', 'off' in 'offer'. Get your child to cut out the smaller words and combine them to make new ones, or arrange them in patterns (for example, line up all the words that start with the same first and second letters).

Breaking up big words into smaller words is a good way of learning how to pronounce words that are new or difficult.

entertainment

Sp ring Col e

leg

IN AT I

FORM ON

MATHEMATICS

Why do schools teach maths?
We all use maths every day, even if that's not what we call it. We check our change at the shops, work out how expensive the new carpet will be, decide when we need to leave the house to get to the airport. And at the other end of the spectrum, brilliant scientists are using maths to build the internet and help us understand the laws of the universe.

TIP How many steps?

Help your child to practise estimating. Find two trees in the park: can your child guess how many strides it would take to walk from one to the other? Walk between the trees, asking your child to count your strides out loud. Stop half way: does your child want to change their guess?

Maths isn't always about calculating exact answers. Being able to estimate a rough answer is an important mathematical skill that helps your child solve problems and check their work.

Teaching for every child

Children are taught about:
▷ **number**: counting, calculating, solving simple problems and making simple lists, tables and charts
▷ **shape, space and measure**: looking at, handling and describing the features of common shapes such as triangles, rectangles, squares, cubes, hexagons, pentagons, cylinders and spheres; describing positions, directions and movements and right angles; working and measuring with units of time, length, weight and capacity.

Using and applying mathematics involves doing practical tasks and talking about mathematical problems. Children are taught to reason about problems and solve them. They communicate their thinking and results using objects, pictures, diagrams, words, numbers and symbols. They estimate and measure everyday items. They do sums in their heads, especially by imagining numbers and the relationships between them.

At this age, children get into the habit of doing maths in their heads, without relying on calculators.

> **The daily mathematics lesson**
> Nearly all schools use the *National Numeracy Strategy: Framework for teaching mathematics*. This gives detailed aims for teaching maths, which is taught during a daily maths lesson for all pupils.

Counting doesn't have to be boring – make it fun for your child. There are all sorts of ways to help them remember how to pronounce numbers and how to put them in the right order.

You and your child could try these:

- count out loose change
- sing counting songs
- count out how many times they can skip a rope.

Keep an eye out for chances to count out loud – it's all great practice for your child.

Some children find it especially tricky to say the numbers from 11 to 19. When your child counts out loud, listen to these numbers. Encourage them to concentrate on the 'teens' if they find them difficult.

	100
	95
	90
	85
	80
	75
	70
	65
	60
	55
	50
	45
	40
	35
	30
	25
	20
	15
	10
	5
	0

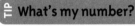

TIP

What's my number?

Think of a number between
1 and 100. Can your child
guess your number in 20
questions or less?

Instead of just making
random guesses, they need
to ask questions that help
them narrow down the
options. Is the number odd?
Is it even? Is it bigger than
20? Smaller than 60?

Your child can cross out
sections of the number line
(right) to help them get
closer to the right answer.
If they use a pencil, you can
use the line several times.

Targets for every child

Around age 7, most children are able to:

Using and applying mathematics
▷ choose a sensible approach to tackle a problem
▷ use words, symbols and simple diagrams to record what they do in a mathematical way
▷ notice patterns and describe them
▷ explain how they solved a problem.

Number
▷ count, read and write whole numbers up to 100, and put them in order
▷ count on or back in ones or tens from different starting numbers
▷ tell if numbers are odd or even
▷ know that you can undo an addition with a subtraction
▷ know by heart all adding and subtracting facts for each number up to ten (for example, know the facts that $6 + 4 = 10$, $10 - 4 = 6$ and $10 - 6 = 4$, $4 + 2 = 6$ and $6 - 4 = 2$, $6 - 2 = 4$, and so on)
▷ know the pairs of numbers in tens that make 100 (for example, $30 + 70 = 100$, $70 + 30 = 100$)
▷ know that they can do addition in any order, and that it's easier to start with the bigger numbers
▷ understand that multiplying is the same as adding more of the same number
▷ double numbers or halve them
▷ know the × 2 and × 10 tables by heart.

Shape, space and measure

▷ use the mathematical names for common two-dimensional and three-dimensional shapes; say how many sides and corners a shape has, and if it has any right angles
▷ predict how a shape would appear in a mirror
▷ recognise turning movements such as whole turns, half turns and quarter turns or right angles
▷ measure or weigh things using units such as centimetres, metres, litres or kilograms; choose sensible units to use
▷ use a ruler to draw and measure lines to the nearest centimetre
▷ tell the time to the half and quarter hour.

Science

Why do schools teach science?

Every child has a natural curiosity about the way the world works: science lessons show how they can get answers to questions such as how plants grow or why it's dark at night.

TIP Catch this!

When you play a ball game with your child, get them to think about the reasons why the ball moves at different speeds. Show them that the harder they throw or kick the ball, the faster it moves.

It works the other way round: can they see that the faster the ball is moving, the harder it is to stop it?

Teaching for every child

Children look at and explore:

▷ *life processes and living things*, such as familiar animals and plants
▷ *materials and their properties*, such as wood, paper and rock
▷ *physical processes*: simple ideas in physics, taught through
  experiences with electricity, forces, light and sounds.

Through work in these three areas children are taught about *scientific enquiry*. The teacher or children ask questions, then the children work together to try to answer the questions by finding things out and recording their work. They think about the tests and comparisons they have done and whether or not these are a fair way to help answer the questions. They find out more about scientific ideas from books and computer sources. And they write and draw (sometimes on computers), communicating their work and their results in scientific language, drawings, charts and tables.

Science

Sink or swim

Bathrooms are full of interesting objects – from bath toys to bars of soap. Get your child to sort different items to see what sinks and what floats. They can arrange all the objects into two groups: sinking things and floating things. What are the sinking things made of? What are the floating things made of?

Some things that float will be made of the same material as things that sink – for example, a plastic duck and a plastic nail scrubbing brush. Can they work out that the duck floats because it's filled with air?

In science your child will learn to think about materials and their properties by observing them and grouping them. This tip helps them to practise both skills.

⚃ Expect the unexpected

You don't need a lab to do a scientific experiment. There are lots of ways you and your child could set up an experiment in your own home.

See how long a plant can stay alive without water. Your child will need to compare two plants of the same kind – but one given water and one not.

Before you start...
Get your child to say what they think will happen to the plant without water.

During the experiment...
Each day, get your child to write down any changes they see.

Afterwards...
Are there any differences between what your child expected would happen and what actually did happen? Talk about what the reasons for these might be (for example, the plant without water might take longer to die than expected – probably because there was already water in it).

Targets for every child

Around age 7, most children are able to:

Scientific enquiry
▷ suggest how they can find out about a scientific question
▷ look for information they need (this might be by looking carefully at the world around them, or by reading something in a book)
▷ think about what they have found out and decide whether this is what they thought would happen
▷ look at and compare objects and living things, and classify them using words such as 'loud' or 'quiet', 'hard' or 'soft', and 'faster' or 'slower'.

Life processes and living things
▷ describe what an animal or plant needs in order to live, and compare it with others by talking about simple features (for example, 'it has six legs, not four')
▷ understand that every living thing eats, grows and reproduces
▷ recognise that different plants and animals are found in different places (for example, ponds and woodland).

Materials and their properties
▷ sort materials into groups, using words to describe their properties such as 'shiny', 'hard' or 'smooth'
▷ describe how some materials change when, for example, they are heated, cooled, stretched or twisted.

Physical processes
▷ make a bulb light up using a simple circuit with a battery and a switch, and see how this is similar to the lights and switches in their home
▷ compare the brightness or colour of lights, and the loudness or pitch of sounds
▷ describe moving objects by talking about speed and direction.

What to wear?

Ask your child to describe the clothes they are wearing. What's the material like – is it thin? Thick? Waterproof? Tough? Why have they chosen to wear those particular clothes – does the choice have something to do with what the weather's like outside?

Get your child to look at the soles of the shoes in your house. Some will be smooth while others might be ridged or bumpy – can your child explain which type would be best in which situation? Talk with your child about the different ways in which clothes keep us comfortable and safe.

Some of the materials used in the clothes may be very simple and traditional – for example, wool. Others, such as plastics, come from modern scientific discoveries. Your child will begin to learn that scientists have looked at the properties of materials in order to invent new ones.

Design and technology

Why do schools teach design and technology?

A video recorder that's easy to programme or a desk that's just right for the home computer … good design makes things easier and more enjoyable to use. Design and technology lessons give children the opportunity to investigate how well familiar products and objects actually work, and who they're really aimed at. By answering questions such as 'Is this the right tool for the job?' they learn how to solve practical problems skilfully, creatively and with imagination.

TIP Make it yourself

Put your child's design and technology skills to creative use in the home. For example, ask them to make festival and birthday cards for friends and relatives. Help them choose the things they will need: scissors, glue, card, pens and pencils, and so on. Pay attention to the techniques your child uses to make the card. Are they folding neatly? Cutting along straight lines? Using the right amount of glue – not too much? A set aim often helps. For example, you could agree with your child that they will create 10 cards over the course of a year, for birthdays, Christmas and so on.

Teaching for every child

Children are taught to:
▷ look at and talk about familiar products (made of materials such as card, textiles and food) to see how they work
▷ practise simple practical skills and do tasks, such as cutting, folding and gluing, which they will use as they make their own products
▷ plan and create their own products, using what they have learned.

For example, they might look at hand and finger puppets, asking questions such as 'How have they been put together? What type of fabric has been used? Who have they been made for?' They then practise skills, such as cutting and joining the kinds of fabrics used in the puppet. Finally they design and make a puppet with a purpose: for example, a finger puppet designed to entertain a smaller brother or sister on a long car journey.

Design and technology

Targets for every child

Around age 7, most children are able to:

▷ develop ideas for design and technology products, talk about these ideas and plan what to do next, using pictures, words and models

▷ choose and safely use the tools, equipment and techniques they need for their ideas

▷ assemble materials and components in different ways

▷ talk about how they could improve their work in future.

TIP The icing on the cake

Next time you make cakes or biscuits, get your child to put the icing on the cake. But first get them to ask the people who will eat the cake what colours or flavours they would like to see. With biscuits, people can also choose shapes and fillings – for example, raisins or cherries.

Design and technology teaches children about food and cooking, but also about making products with people in mind. By finding out what people want, your child will make sure that the cakes or biscuits meet a need.

Games such as 'I-spy'
or 'animal, vegetable,
mineral' help children
to look carefully at the
world around them and
see what materials things
are made of. In the home,
you can get your child to
look for all the things
made of plastic, wood
or rubber. Now that they
have spotted them, do
they all have a function
in common? For example,
everything made of rubber
might need to stretch or
flex at some point.

Design and technology

Information and communication technology

Why do schools teach information and communication technology?
You can email through your TV, surf the internet from a mobile phone, or do the shopping from your home computer: modern technology is changing the way we live and work. And children need to learn how to manage it all — how to get hold of information, store it, share it with others and tailor it to their own needs. That's where their information and communication technology (ICT) lessons come in. This is where they learn how to use the internet and email, digital cameras and scanners, recording equipment and computer software.

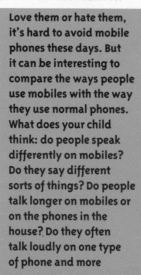

> ## TIP 'I'm on the train ...'
>
> Love them or hate them, it's hard to avoid mobile phones these days. But it can be interesting to compare the ways people use mobiles with the way they use normal phones. What does your child think: do people speak differently on mobiles? Do they say different sorts of things? Do people talk longer on mobiles or on the phones in the house? Do they often talk loudly on one type of phone and more quietly on the other? Ask your child if they can think of reasons for the differences. See if your child can tell you some of the advantages and disadvantages of both types of phone.
>
> *Some researchers think that mobile phones may be unsafe, especially for children under the age of 16. As a precaution, the government has advised schools that it is best for children only to use mobile phones in an emergency.*

Teaching for every child

Children learn how to use ICT to find out information, and then to share and exchange it. They become familiar with some hardware and software – for example, learning how to use a word processor and 'paint' software. They store information on computers, present it in different ways, and talk about how ICT can be used both in and out of school.

Targets for every child

Around age 7, most children are able to:

▷ use ICT to handle information in different ways, including gathering it, organising it, storing it, and presenting it to others

▷ start to feel comfortable using computer software in their everyday work (for example, they might write and change their class work using a word processor or other computer packages and make use of graphics and sound)

▷ use programmable toys, putting together computerised instructions in the right order

▷ explore what happens using ICT.

At school your child will learn to use computer software to improve the presentation of their work. They will see that they can take the same information (words), but by presenting it in different styles and sizes, they can make it more powerful and dramatic. Get them to look at the different typefaces on this page. Which do they like best? Which make the words clear, and which make them look confusing?

Information and communication technology

43

History

Why do schools teach history?
How did we get here? Where do we come from? History helps shed light on these big questions. It introduces children to an unfamiliar but important world – the past. Piecing together the picture of the past is a bit like detective work. Children use different kinds of evidence to find out about people's lives and events and how things have changed. Learning how to weigh up evidence and reach conclusions are just some of the skills children develop through studying the history of Britain and the wider world. As they do this, they begin to understand and remember a framework of significant events and people.

TIP Spot the difference

You may not consider yourself 'history' just yet, but it can be very useful for your child to compare their own life with yours. Talk with your child about the sort of things you did when you were their age. What's different, and what's the same?

If you keep photo albums, look through them with your child. Looking at the earlier pictures, can your child spot any differences between now and then? Are the clothes different compared with now? What about types of car, kitchens or gardens?

Teaching for every child

In history children learn to place events in chronological order, and about the lives of men, women and children from the history of Britain and the wider world. They also look at significant events, such as Remembrance Day or the Olympic Games. They use books and other sources to help them ask and answer questions. They listen to stories and respond to them. They learn how the past is different from the present and ask: how have I changed? How has life changed for my parents, or others around me?

TIP What's new, what's old?

On a journey to school
or to the shops, get your
child to look at some of
the buildings on the way.
Ask them to point out some
old buildings and some
that are more recent. Can
your child explain why they
think a building is old or
new, or how it has changed?
Get them to look out for
other clues about the past
such as street and shop
signs, types of pillar boxes
and phone booths, statues
and memorials.

Targets for every child

Around age 7, most children are able to:

▷ use words about the passing of time (such as before, after, a long time ago, in the past) and put events in order

▷ realise that some things happened before anyone living now was born

▷ begin to recognise why people acted as they did and why some events happened

▷ understand that their own lives are different from those of people in the past

▷ ask questions about the past and answer them by talking to people, reading books, looking at photographs, handling objects, using computer sources or by visiting museums and historical sites

▷ see that the past has been represented in different ways and talk about some of these ways.

TIP What happened next?

After you read a story with your child, talk with them about what happened in it. Can your child remember the order of the main events? Try to get your child to think about the reasons why a main character in the story acted as they did. Would they have done the same thing in their position? If they had acted differently, would the story have had a different ending?

In history, children think about events and how they are linked together. Discussing stories in this way practises the same skill.

This tip works best with true or fairly realistic stories.

History

Geography

Why do schools teach geography?

We all make a mark on where we live, and where we live leaves its mark
on us. Learning about the links between our lives and the environment
around us is central to geography lessons at this stage. Children find out
about an area in the UK and how it compares with other places around the
world. To help them get the best out of their investigations inside and outside
the classroom, they learn how to use maps, photographs and computers —
skills which prove useful in other subjects as well as when they leave school.

TIP What's it called?

Take your child to a
window or a high point
with a view. Get them to
describe what they can
see. Can they tell which
features are natural and
which have been put
there by people?

*Words such as 'house',
'bridge', 'road', 'stream',
and 'river' are good
geographical vocabulary
for your child to use.*

Teaching for every child

Children learn to use geographical skills, and resources including maps and plans, to find out about places:
▷ where features are located (for example, shops, bus stops, streams and trees)
▷ how and why features change (for example, heavy rain causing floods)
▷ how to care for the environment.

At this age they do this through their study of:
▷ the immediate neighbourhood of the school and the school's own buildings and grounds
▷ a similar-sized area, either in the UK or overseas, that is different from the area in and around their school.

Targets for every child

Around age 7, most children are able to:

▷ describe the main features of places they study, using geographical words like 'hill', 'river', 'motorway'

▷ understand how places may be similar to and different from each other

▷ recognise where things are and why they are there (for example, why a pedestrian crossing is on one part of a road rather than another)

▷ spot changes in the places they study

▷ see how people affect the environment

▷ find out about places by observing them, asking and answering questions and using other resources such as maps and photographs

▷ give their views about places.

TIP Food search

Food in our kitchens has been imported from countries all over the world. Pick out some packets of food from your kitchen cupboard and ask your child to find out where each came from by reading the label. Once your child has a list of places, both here and overseas, get them to find out where these places are by using a map, an atlas or a globe.

Out and about

The next time you are in
the park with your child,
get them to have a close
look around. Can they
describe the park's main
features – for example,
trees, hill, football pitch,
tennis court? Has anything
about the park changed
recently?

Ask your child what
they like about the park
and what they don't like.
What would they do to
make the park a better
place, both for children
and for adults?

Art and design

Why do schools teach art and design?

There's nothing like discovering your favourite colours in a box of paints when you're a child. You can show how you see the world by making a picture of what's around you or communicating how you feel, using different patterns, materials and textures. Children feed their imagination through art and design. They study different sorts of art work, from murals to sculptures, and learn how art, craft and design enrich their lives and ours.

TIP Thoughts and feelings

Practical objects, such as furniture, can also be attractive and appealing. Get your child to talk about the different kinds of furniture to sit on that you have in your home: kitchen chairs, easy chairs, stools and sofas. What is each chair for? Which pattern and colour is your child's favourite, and why? Which is most relaxing? Do they have a chair they like to daydream in?

An important part of art and design is exploring feelings. Artists think about what kind of feelings different colours, textures and patterns create – excitement, calm, curiosity and so on.

Teaching for every child

Children are taught to:
- explore and develop their ideas by recording what they see and imagine, and by asking and answering questions about it
- try out different materials, tools and techniques (such as painting, printmaking, modelling clay)
- review their own and others' work, saying what they think and feel about it
- work with colour, pattern and texture, line and tone, shape, form and space
- find out about differences and similarities in the work of artists, craftspeople and designers in different times and cultures.

They do this on their own and working with others, using a range of starting points (such as their own experiences, natural and made objects, the local environment) and looking at a range of work (for example, during visits to galleries, on the internet).

Targets for every child

Around age 7, most children are able to:
▷ explore and express ideas in colour, shape, form and space
▷ experiment with a variety of materials, tools and techniques
▷ comment on differences in others' work, and suggest ways of improving their own work.

TIP

Collect it!

Don't throw away those sketches and doodles your child draws – they might come in useful at school. Get your child into the habit of collecting any art work they do in their spare time, as well as any pictures and patterns they like or find inspiring. These could be drawings, photographs, newspaper and magazine clippings, textiles or even leaves and flowers.

Your child could label cereal boxes to store themes – for example, 'people', 'patterns' and 'places'.

It's tempting to help your child when they are drawing a picture. But hold back. Talk to your child about what they have drawn and help them to focus on those parts that are more detailed, realistic or expressive – so that they can build on their own strengths. Praise, give feedback, and encourage them to look again. One of the key skills in drawing is hand–eye co-ordination.

Anything you can do that encourages your child to look first, then draw, and then look again, will strengthen their art work.

Art and design

Music

Why do schools teach music?

We've all got our 'desert island discs', songs that remind us of places we've visited, or tunes that always cheer us up when we're feeling down. Making music together helps children to explore and express their thoughts and feelings. Learning songs from times gone by or from different parts of the world helps children learn about other times and other cultures. And getting to grips with listening carefully is going to help them in all sorts of different lessons throughout their school career.

TIP Sing it with me

Most children love singing at this age. Give them lots of encouragement – singing is not only fun, but will give your child a sense of melody that will help their school work.

Some songs can also be very helpful for other subjects such as English and mathematics. Remembering songs – like 'Now I know my ABC' or '1, 2, 3, 4, 5, once I caught a fish alive' – can be great for helping your child learn the letters of the alphabet, or to count out numbers.

Teaching for every child

Children are taught how to sing and play musical instruments. They explore sounds and create their own short compositions. They learn to listen carefully, finding out and describing how sounds can change: for example, getting higher, lower, louder, quieter. They experience a wide range of music from different times and cultures.

Targets for every child

Around age 7, most children are able to:

▷ sing songs from memory, knowing when the tune goes up and down
▷ keep to a steady rhythm when singing and playing music
▷ start making their own simple musical patterns, carefully choosing different sounds
▷ describe sounds using words such as 'high' and 'low', and by using musical symbols
▷ improve their own work.

TIP · Keep to the beat

Children find rhythm easier when they link it with physical movement. Help your child to feel rhythms in different ways. You could both clap along to music on the radio, or your child could skip with a rope in time to music.

Give your child a chance to
listen to lots of different
types of music. Try to play
as wide a range as possible
in the home, so they can
begin to choose what
they prefer to listen to
at different times.

Music isn't just about
sound – silence is also very
important to music. Help
your child to appreciate
silence, encouraging them
to listen to the kind of quiet
background sounds we
might hear when everything
else is turned off. Find a
time when you can switch
off the TV, turn off the radio,
unplug the phone. They may
find it a new and strange
experience!

Music

PHYSICAL EDUCATION

Why do schools teach PE?
Whether regular exercise is swimming or a Sunday afternoon kickaround, we know keeping fit is important these days. In physical education, or PE, children learn that it's fun to stay in shape. They learn how to prepare for and recover from exercise, and what happens to their body when they work out in a variety of ways. It's a vital foundation to help them lead active and healthy lives as they grow up.

Teaching for every child

Dance: children learn how to move rhythmically and expressively, showing their imagination.
Games: they learn how to use their skills to score points or goals against others.
Gymnastics: they learn how to link together, accurately:
▷ movements
▷ still shapes
▷ balances.

Children are taught how to follow rules, and how to move and play safely. They learn how to work on their own and with others. They work together in teams, competing against others.

TIP

A hop and a skip

Here's a simple physical movement that helps with lots of PE activities. Try getting your child to progress from hopping to skipping:

• get them to hop for three paces on one leg, then hop for three on the other leg. How smoothly can they make the transition between the two?

• get your child to alternate hop–step–hop–step. Once they can move easily from hop to step, in a fluid movement, they are skipping.

Targets for every child

Around age 7, most children are able to:
▷ remember and repeat skills, performing them with control and co-ordination
▷ choose the right skills for what they are doing so that they can:
  * use tactics in simple games to score points against an opponent
  * make up and perform short gymnastic sequences that join actions together
  * move in time to a beat, showing their ideas and feelings in short dances
▷ pick out and copy actions, describing what they and others do well, and suggesting how to improve them
▷ describe how their bodies feel in different activities (for example, if they run a lot, their heart will beat faster and they will get hot)
▷ enjoy being physically active.

> Most schools will aim to make sure that the time your child spends exercising at school – including PE and any out-of-hours sports – adds up to about two hours per week.

TIP
Throw and catch

Children are often tempted to duck from a ball coming towards them. But there are two easy ways to help them practise catching without wanting to duck:
* they can practise by bouncing the ball off a wall
* throw the ball to them, but make sure it bounces (not more than waist-high) before they have to catch it.
To succeed, they need to watch the ball all the time.

Get moving

Active parents make a big
impression on children at
this age. Your child is more
likely to be active in later
life if they get the habit
with you at an early age.

Religious education

Why do schools teach religious education?
To be able to understand their own beliefs and values, children need to learn about and respond to the beliefs and values of others. In religious education (RE) children learn about the main religions in this country, particularly Christianity. Teachers aim to help children respect the beliefs and practices of others as well as discover more about their own.

Your child's school must teach religious education, but there is no national programme of study. For most schools, RE teaching will be based on a local education authority programme. Some schools (for example, church schools) may follow a different programme. The local programme is shaped by national guidelines. These say that teaching should:
▷ reflect the fact that the religious traditions in Great Britain are mainly Christian
▷ also include teaching about the other important religions in this country.

There are no targets for RE at key stage 1.

If you think it is best for your child, you can take them out of all or part of religious education lessons.

Teaching for every child

Children are taught about the stories, festivals and events that help to provide the pattern and meaning to their lives. Teachers encourage children to talk and write about the variety of ceremonies, buildings and people, in Christianity and other religions. Children learn to think about these and put forward their own ideas about them. For example, children are taught about the celebration and meaning of Christmas.

Tell me a story

Searching for new stories to read? Look in a library or bookshop for children's highlights from Christian, Jewish, Islamic, Hindu, Sikh and Buddhist traditions. There are many exciting stories that offer plenty to talk about.

Religious education

Look up and around

Take a look at different religious buildings (for example, a cathedral, a mosque) when you are out for the day or on holiday. Point out the different shapes, colours and sounds. See if you can collect any leaflets that give you more information about the building.

Help your child draw and colour the symbols of the main religions in Britain, given below. They can choose a symbol, draw it at the top of a large sheet of paper, and then collect and stick on pictures of:

- people carrying out traditions or rituals from that religion
- the sacred books of that religion.

If some of the symbols are unfamiliar, a dictionary or encyclopaedia will tell you more about them.

Judaism
Star of David

Islam
Crescent Moon

Christianity
The Cross

Hinduism
Aum

Buddhism
Dharma Wheel

Sikhism
The Khanda

Religious education

Personal, social and health education and citizenship

Why do schools teach personal, social and health education (PSHE) and citizenship?

To lead independent, happy lives, children must develop their self-confidence. This involves taking responsibility for their own health and well-being. In this subject, children learn about these important life skills. They learn not only about their own rights, duties and responsibilities but also about the rights and responsibilities of others. Teaching aims to help them respect and value the richness and diversity of our society.

Primary schools do not have to teach PSHE and citizenship, but the government encourages them to do so. It might not be taught as a subject in its own right – it could be taught:
▷ through other subjects
▷ through special time set aside
▷ by creating special opportunities for children to take responsibility.

There are no targets for PSHE and citizenship at key stage 1.

Teaching for every child

Children are taught *personal skills*, such as how to:
▷ be more independent and confident
▷ see what their strengths are
▷ think about what's fair and unfair, right and wrong
▷ set themselves goals, and try to achieve them
▷ keep themselves safe and healthy.

Children also learn *social skills*:
▷ they think about what kind of groups they belong to, and how they contribute to them
▷ they learn that it is important to respect others and get on with them.

Schools look for opportunities to teach these skills and ideas in everyday life. For example, your child might learn about their strengths through doing classroom jobs. They might discuss classroom rules with other children and the teacher. And in science, they will learn simple hygiene rules such as the importance of washing their hands.

TIP Look both ways

When crossing the road with your child, let them look to see if it's safe. (It's easier, and often quicker, to decide when to cross yourself and say 'let's go now', but sometimes it's better to let your child take responsibility.)

Personal, social and health education and citizenship

TIP It's good to talk

As you talk to your child about what they've done at school, get them to go through their successes and achievements, and also the areas they are finding difficult. How do they know they are doing well in the successful areas? How will they know when they're succeeding in the difficult areas?

Sex and relationship education and drugs education

Your child's school has to provide a written statement about its sex and relationship education (SRE) policy. This will say whether SRE will be taught and, if so, from what age. It will also explain what will be covered. The National Curriculum for science says that between the ages of 5 and 7 your child should learn that all animals, including humans, reproduce.

Schools:
▷ should consult parents when forming SRE policy
▷ view their work as supporting parents with SRE, not doing it for them
▷ are expected to protect children from inappropriate teaching and materials, in line with their age and cultural backgrounds, and ensure children learn about marriage.

In the National Curriculum for science children learn that some drugs can be good for the body (medicines) and others harmful (prohibited drugs). At this age many schools use teaching about personal, social and health education and citizenship to help children think about treating others with consideration and resisting unwanted pressure – important foundations for later teaching about SRE and drugs education.

The Education Act 1996 gives you the right to withdraw your child from all or part of sex education lessons. However, the law doesn't allow you to withdraw your child from the relevant aspects of science teaching.

Help your body

Different parts of the body need special care and attention. Can your child name parts of the body that need protection, and how? For example:
• in sunny weather we should use sun cream to look after our skin
• on a walk, a pair of sturdy shoes comes in handy to stop our feet getting sore and wet.

 *(side text)* Personal, social and health education and citizenship

Help!
Answers to questions

This book says that most children reach the 'target for every child' by age 7. But I'm worried that my child won't.
In the key stage I section of this book, the 'targets for every child' in each subject describe what children should be able to know and do. Level 2 is the target for 7 year olds.

The aim of the targets is to give a level that most children should have reached by a certain age. There will always be some children below and others beyond the target.

If your child finds their work easy, talk to their teacher about which target they should be aiming for – they may need to aim higher. If your child is likely to find level 2 hard when they get to age 7, the school will tell you in good time. Every school must give parents an annual report on how their child is progressing in each National Curriculum subject. (The school is not obliged by law to give a level for each subject in this annual report, but some will.)

You may hear your child's teacher talking about level 2a, 2b or 2c. These are finer divisions of the level: 2a is high, 2c is low. If your child achieves level 2c at age 7, they will have to work hard to reach level 4 by the time they are aged II.

If the school says that your child is likely to find it hard to reach the target, remember:
  ▷ children develop at different rates. Some may not reach the level at the given age, but will catch up later
  ▷ at the moment, however, your child may need extra help from their school and from you. Talk to their teacher about how you can help.

What if my child has special educational needs?

Help is available. For more information, see page 82.

Where can I find help if my child has health or social problems at school?

School is about much more than learning: it's about your child growing up, making friends, growing in confidence. School might bring all kinds of questions: for example, what kind of uniform do you need to buy? If your child has asthma, how can the school help? This book focuses on learning between the ages of 3 and 7, and doesn't try to look at the other questions in detail. But on page 83 you will find out where you can go for help with the other questions.

I see there are tips in this guide, but I don't have time to do them all – will my child be left behind?

No. The tips in this guide are there for you to complement the work of the school. Do as many tips as you feel able to do, but don't feel guilty about those you can't. The main thing is always to show an interest in what your child is learning at school. (But remember – even if you don't have time to do some tips, grandparents are often pleased to help.)

My child seems to have difficulty keeping up at school and finds the work difficult. What can I do?

Talk regularly to your child's teacher. You don't have to wait for a parents' evening: you can ask the school for an appointment with your child's teacher at any time. Find out more about what your child is doing at school and ask the teacher what your child could do at home to help their learning at school. See also 'special educational needs' on page 82.

My child's school doesn't seem to be teaching all the subjects in this guide. Why?

Primary schools have to teach all but one of the subjects explained in this guide. Schools must teach religious education and all the National Curriculum subjects. Schools are expected to teach a daily literacy hour, a daily maths lesson, and PE every week. But:

▷ schools don't have to teach the other subjects every week. As long as they cover the curriculum, it is up to them. So your child's school might teach some subjects in blocks

▷ schools don't have to call the subjects by the names in this guide. For example, they might teach some geography and history together and give it a more child-friendly name, such as 'our neighbourhood'.

Personal, social and health education and citizenship is an optional subject.

I hear a lot about the literacy hour and the daily mathematics lesson. What are they?

These are teaching methods set out in the National Literacy Strategy and National Numeracy Strategy, which give detailed aims for teaching most of the English curriculum, and all of the maths curriculum. For more information, send for the two free leaflets below (call the DfEE orderline on 08000 96 66 26 to ask for a copy).

I see there are national tests only in English and maths. Does this mean the other subjects are less important?

All the National Curriculum subjects are very important: they all contribute to your child's education in different ways. The National Curriculum was introduced to make sure that all children are given a broad and balanced education. PE, for example, contributes to your child's physical development. Art and design and music give your child other experiences that help them to develop important skills, such as being creative.

What is a home–school agreement?

Your child's school should give you a written home–school agreement, setting out the school's aims and values. The agreement will list the school's responsibilities, your responsibilities, and what the school expects of its pupils. Each school's agreement is different but all should cover the importance of regular and punctual attendance, discipline and good behaviour, and homework.

Your support and encouragement are very important to your child's progress and the home–school agreement will help you to work with the school. Schools have to review their agreements every two or three years and must consult parents before making any changes. You will be asked to sign a copy of the agreement. If you don't feel you can sign it, you don't have to. Please talk to the school about it.

Help Answers to questions

Will my child be taught sex and relationship education?
This depends on the school's policy. Find out more on page 71 of this book.

Should I help my child with their homework?
▷ Take advice from your child's teacher about how much help you should give with the work itself. Depending on your child, it may be helpful to give them a hand with particular homework tasks. But an important aim of homework is to help children learn how to work independently, so it is helpful to encourage them, but not to do the work for them.
▷ If you haven't got a copy of the school's homework policy, do ask for one and check what it has to say.
▷ Make sure your child has a quiet space to do homework in, and help them to plan their time.

My child just wants to watch television instead of doing homework. Help!
Television can encourage learning if chosen carefully. For example, some wildlife documentaries are excellent introductions to important topics in science and geography. Schools don't always have time to show these kinds of television programmes in full. So if your child watches them, this will add to their school learning. In this guide you will find tips that make good use of television – often in ways that encourage your child to note or discuss what they see.

However, homework is important and sometimes it may be demanding. On many occasions it will be best simply to turn the TV off (or video the programme!), and give your child both encouragement and support when they are not motivated.

Here are some of the words and phrases you may hear teachers use – and what they mean.

attainment target

Each National Curriculum subject has one or more attainment targets. Attainment targets help teachers decide how well children have learned what they have been taught. Each attainment target is made up of eight level descriptions and 'exceptional performance'. They are a kind of measure. Each level is like the rung of a ladder – children should move up through the level descriptions as they grow older and make progress (see the diagram on page 10). The main part of this book includes summaries of level 2, the target for 7 year olds.

baseline assessment

When your child starts school, the teacher will look at what they can do, so that they can record a starting point for your child's learning. This is called baseline assessment, and it is described on page 15. There is more information in the free DfEE leaflet *Is your child about to start school?* (Ring the DfEE orderline 08000 96 66 26 to ask for a copy.)

Is your child about to start school?

breadth

The National Curriculum handbook for teachers has a section for each subject called 'breadth of study'. This says that your child is entitled to be taught through a range of important learning experiences. For example:

▷ between the ages of 5 and 7, in science, your child should – among other things – carry out complete experiments
▷ between the ages of 7 and 11, in music, your child should use computers to record and alter sounds.

These deepen and broaden your child's experience of the subject.

English as an additional language (EAL)

Children who speak English as an additional language, rather than as their first language, may need extra help with their reading and writing. They will need lots of opportunities to talk with English-speaking adults and children about their work, thoughts and feelings. Often what they need most is varied, vibrant teaching that involves visual resources, sound, speaking and writing to make it easier for them to learn English. Some children for whom English is an additional language may also have special educational needs.

inclusion

One of the aims of the government is that, as far as possible, schools should teach all children the National Curriculum, whatever their needs. This includes children with special educational needs and those who are extremely gifted and talented (who need harder challenges to tackle), together with other pupils.

ICT

This stands for information and communication technology, which includes the use of computers, the internet, and video and sound recording equipment. This subject used to be called 'information technology'.

key stage

A key stage is a block of years in your child's schooling. Key stage 1 covers the first two years your child spends at school (aged 5–7), key stage 2 the next four (aged 7–11), key stage 3 ages 11–14, and key stage 4 ages 14–16. See the diagram on page 7.

levels (level descriptions)
Each level is a measure teachers use to check how much your child knows, understands, and can do. See 'attainment target' above and the diagram on page 10.

National Literacy Strategy (NLS)
This is an important piece of government guidance to primary schools, giving detailed aims for teaching reading and writing. These are taught in a daily literacy hour.

National Numeracy Strategy (NNS)
This is an important piece of government guidance to primary schools, giving detailed aims for teaching maths, which is taught in a daily maths lesson.

programme of study
Every National Curriculum subject has a programme of study. This sets out what your child is entitled to be taught in school. The main part of this book summarises the programmes of study and the attainment targets (see above).

PSHE
Personal, social and health education. See page 68.

'SATs'
Many people call **National Curriculum tests and tasks** by the name of 'SATs'. The diagram on page 7 shows when children take these compulsory tests. Some schools use **National Curriculum optional tests** in other years, to track children's progress.

Help! Answers to questions

Special educational needs (SEN)

Children have special educational needs if they have learning difficulties that make it much harder for them to learn than most children of the same age. SEN includes children with a range of physical or sensory difficulties, emotional and behavioural difficulties or difficulties with speech, language or social interaction. These children may need to be helped more than other children of the same age, and perhaps in different ways. If you think your child has SEN your first step should be to talk to your child's class teacher. Every school will also have a Special Educational Needs Coordinator (SENCO) who will be able to provide more advice about how you and the school can help your child.

There is more information in the free DfEE leaflet *Special educational needs – a guide for parents*. (Ring the DfEE orderline on 08000 96 66 26 to ask for a copy.)

year 1, year 2 (etc)

Because children in a school year have birthdays in different months, it is simpler for schools not to talk about the year by referring to the age of the children in it. Instead, they talk about the number of years since children began key stage 1. See the diagram on page 7.

For more help on many topics

This book is about what your child will learn at school. Of course, there are many other issues to do with your child's education, health and well-being that don't link directly to the curriculum. Your child's school is always your first point of contact for help.

The DfEE has set up a web site for parents, which also has lots of useful resources. You can find it at **http://www.parents.dfee.gov.uk**, and it has two main sections.

In School covers:
 ▷ literacy and numeracy, with more about the curriculum
 ▷ school activity charges
 ▷ exams and assessments
 ▷ school reports
 ▷ parents' evenings
 ▷ types of school
 ▷ attendance
 ▷ discipline and exclusions
 ▷ school administration (governors and LEAs)
 ▷ school security
 ▷ school meals and milk
 ▷ home–school agreements
 ▷ gifted and talented children
 ▷ special educational needs
 ▷ English as an additional language.

Out of School covers:
 ▷ choosing a school, and the admissions process
 ▷ school travel and transport
 ▷ learning at home, including ways to learn on the internet
 ▷ revision and homework
 ▷ health and welfare, including bullying, pupil health, smoking and drugs
 ▷ pre-school education and childcare
 ▷ further education
 ▷ higher education
 ▷ work experience and careers
 ▷ adult learning
 ▷ support groups for parents and carers.

The web site's **School Search** also lets you look for schools by name or postcode, and see:
▷ their performance table results
▷ Ofsted reports
▷ the school's own web site, if they have one.

Places to Go will look for events and attractions in your area for your child – from museums to pop concerts. The web site also has lots of links to resources on the internet, which can help your child's learning.

One of these is the DfEE's **Discover** site, where you can find leaflets about different National Curriculum topics – for example, 'Romans' or 'electricity'. They have more of the kind of tips given in this book, with suggestions of places to go as well. Your school may give you copies when your child does a certain topic, or you can print them out yourself. You can find them at **http://www.parents.dfee.gov.uk/discover.**

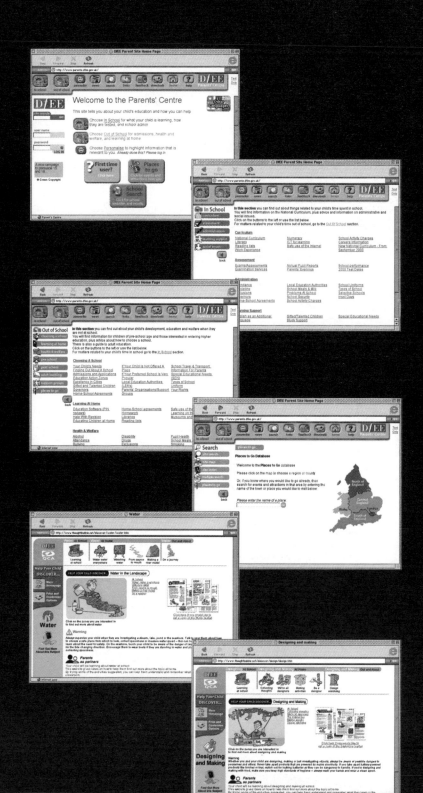

Choosing Childcare:
What to Look For –
Top Ten Questions To Ask

*Investing in
our future*

D/EE
Department for
Education and Employment

Early years

Do you know what's
available for your child?

*Investing in
our future*

How is your
child doing
at school?

D/EE
Department for
Education and Employment

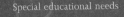

Special educational needs

a guide for parents

DFE
DEPARTMENT FOR
EDUCATION

MATHS YEAR 2000

...four

...three potato...

...two potato...

...one potato...

It all **adds up**

1 bag is 30p... how many troops for £2.10?

D/EE
Department for
Education and Employment

Helping your children with numeracy

A Safer Journey to School

A guide to school travel plans for parents, teachers and governors

TRANSPORT
2000
trust

DETR

SAFE ROUTES
TO SCHOOLS

OUR
HEALTHIER
NATION

D/EE

Read
me

A little reading
goes a long way

Helping with your children's reading

D/EE

Is your child
about to
start school?

This leaflet gives you information
about baseline assessment.

Baseline assessment is what teachers
use to find out children's learning
needs when they start school.

Home-School Agreements

What every parent should know

SCHOOL ATTENDANCE:
INFORMATION FOR PARENTS

If you don't have access to the internet, you can get hold of many useful, free leaflets – the most important ones are listed below. They can all be ordered by calling the DfEE orderline on 08000 96 66 26.

Foundation stage
Early years – do you know what's available for your child?

Your child's progress at school
Is your child about to start school? (about baseline assessment)
How is your child doing at school?* (about national tests and teacher assessment)

English
Learning to read and write at home and at school*
A little reading goes a long way – helping with your children's reading*

Maths
It all adds up – helping your children with numeracy*
Learning about mathematics at home and at school*

Special educational needs
Special educational needs – a guide for parents*
SEN tribunal – how to appeal*
If you have a complaint – SEN tribunal*

Home–school agreements
Home–school agreements – what every parent should know*

Bullying, truancy, health and safety
Bullying – don't suffer in silence (for parents)
Bullying – don't suffer in silence (for children)
School attendance: information for parents*
A safer journey to school: a guide to school travel plans for parents, teachers and governors

If a publication is marked with an asterisk* it is available in other languages and formats, such as Arabic, audio cassette, Bengali, braille, Chinese, Greek, Gujerati, Hindi, Somali, Turkish, Urdu, Vietnamese, Welsh. Not all publications are available in all languages – you can find out which from the orderline.